Self-Portrait in the River of Déjà Vu

Self-Portrait in the River of Déjà Vu

poems

Susan Laughter Meyers

Press 53
Winston-Salem

Press 53, LLC
PO Box 30314
Winston-Salem, NC 27130

First Edition

Copyright © 2019 by Ishmael Blue Meyers

All rights reserved, including the right of reproduction in whole or in part in any form except in the case of brief quotations embodied in critical articles or reviews. For permission, contact publisher at editor@Press53.com, or at the address above.

Cover design by Kevin Morgan Watson

Cover art, "From Her Hat of Goldfinches,"
Copyright © 2017 by Kit Loney

Author photo by Blue Meyers

Library of Congress Control Number
2019933523

Printed on acid-free paper
ISBN 978-1-950413-00-3

to Aunt Mary Alice

*I know the answer, unbreakable.
Ask me again.*

*I don't know half the answer.
No one does, no one did. No one*

*answer. What made us think
there was one question?*

> —from "Finding Her Huck Embroidery
> Folded in a Drawer"

. . . waiting for Blue

> —from "Outside Clinton's Barber
> & Styling Shop"

Acknowledgments

Much appreciation goes to the editors of these journals for first publishing the following poems, sometimes in a different version:

Adanna Literary Journal: Contemporary Love Poems: "Her One and Only" (published as *"beautiful he"*)

American Poetry Journal: "For All Anyone Knows"

Crazyhorse: "Anatomy of a Drowning," "You Offer Apology"

Fall Lines: "Her Purse Is a Room for Sleeping"

The Frank Martin Review: "Dress of Flame & Upside-Down Bird"

Iodine Poetry Journal: "Anniversary Song," "Stitchery & the Child"

Jasper: The Word on Columbia Arts: "Late Summer"

North Carolina Literary Review: "Anointed Yet Badly Blessed," "If Not Birds Dodging Loneliness," "Rain," "Ringwood"

One: "Anytime Soon, Fall"

Prime Number Magazine: "The Body"

South85: "[Lately when sorrows come]"

Southern Poetry Review: "A Little Wildness"

The Southern Review: "[Let's say you forgot me]," "Not one single further sorrow," *"(Now Again) I Am Calling Out,"* "She Could Have Been a Planter Woman" (published as "Planter Woman"), "Weave Such Days to a Whole"

"For All Anyone Knows" appeared on Verse Daily.

"Namesake" was a finalist in the 2008 Porter Fleming Literary Competition.

"[Let's say you forgot me]," "Not one single further sorrow," and *"(Now Again) I Am Calling Out"* are recorded in *The Southern Review* winter 2013 audio gallery.

"If Not Birds Dodging Loneliness" was published in *The Southern Poetry Anthology, Volume VII: North Carolina* (Texas Review Press, 2014), series ed. William Wright.

"Train Headed South" was published in the anthology *What Matters* (Jacar Press, 2013), eds. Debra Kaufman, Richard Krawiec, and Stephanie Levin.

"Lately She Falls to Dreaming" was a part of the 2014 Columbia Broadside Project as a collaboration with visual artist Matt Catoe. "Loosed to Canter the Wild" was a part of the 2015 Columbia Broadside Project as a collaboration with visual artist Lese Corrigan.

"You Offer Apology" was published in *The Manifesto Project* (University of Akron Press, 2016), eds. Alan Michael Parker and Rebecca Hazelton.

"Rain" was the winner of the 2013 James Applewhite Poetry Prize, sponsored by *North Carolina Literary Review*. "Anointed Yet Badly Blessed," "If Not Birds Dodging Loneliness," and "Ringwood" were finalists for this prize in previous years.

"The Body" was published in the anthology *Prime Number Magazine, Editors' Selections, Volume 1* (Press 53, 2012), eds. Clifford GArstang, Valerie Nieman, and Tracy Crow.

Contents

Introduction	xi
Tributes	xiii
Foreword by Alan Michael Parker	xix

I.

For All Anyone Knows	3
Stitchery & the Child	4
Finding Her Huck Embroidery Folded in a Drawer	5
(Now Again) I Am Calling Out	6
[on good days you would]	7
Namesake	8
Under the Waning Moon	9
Stars-on-the-River Tanka	10
Beast with no name	11
Obbligato: Her Faithless Muse	12
She Could Have Been a Planter Woman	13
The Art of Beginning	14
Ringwood	15
The Last Summer with Her Sisters: What to Wear	16
Dress of Flame & Upside-Down Bird	17
The Last Summer with Her Sisters: A Day of Barking	18
Mary Alice Alarm	19
[Let's say you forgot me]	20

II.

Aunt Mary Alice Teaches Me to Tat	23
Mary Alice Tanka	24
If Not Birds Dodging Loneliness	26
Abstractionists & Love: The Art of Forgetting	27
The Last Summer with Her Sisters: Swedish Weaving	29
A Little Wildness	30
The Last Summer with Her Sisters: Long Past Sunup	31
Hearsay	32

Sundog Sonnet	33
Late Summer	34
Why My Heart Has Renamed Itself Mercy	35
Sonata of Tomatoes	36
Why My Heart Has Renamed Itself Shock Therapy	37
Anytime Soon, Fall	38
Her Evening with Monet	39
The Last Summer with Her Sisters: A Dervish of Sand	40
Weave Such Days to a Whole	41
Train Headed South	42
Lately She Falls to Dreaming	43
Her One and Only	44
First Sign of Bad Weather	45
Burial Notes	46
Detective Notes	47
Farewell Meditation	48
I Open the Door	49

III.

Anniversary Song	53
Anointed Yet Badly Blessed	54
You Offer Apology	55
Anatomy of a Drowning	56
Her Purse Is a Room for Sleeping	57
Spirits on the River	58
The Blue of What Remains	59
[Lately when sorrows come]	60
The Body	61
Postcard from Paris, a Deciphering	62
Self-Portrait as a Small Journey	63
Anatomy of a Supposed Life Undrowned	64
Not one single further sorrow	65
Rain	66
Loosed to Canter the Wild	67
Her Only	68

Notes	71
About the Author	73

Introduction

Self-Portrait in the River of Déjà Vu is the fourth and final book by Susan Laughter (pronounced Law-ter) Meyers, who suffered a stroke and died in June of 2017. To family and friends, Susan's death felt impossible, unthinkable, and unendurable. She had been such a vibrant, healthy person. We are still trying to come to terms with our loss.

Most likely every poet in the Carolinas knew Susan from her books, her readings, her workshops, and her service to the poetry community. She traveled widely throughout the Southeast to hear, study, and teach poetry. Not only was Susan a very fine poet, she was loved. The books of so many poets grew from her nurturing. Her archives are housed at Furman University in Greenville, South Carolina. Her enormous personal library was given to schools, libraries, and close friends.

From the beginning Susan's family called her Susan, though her birth certificate reads Alice Susan Laughter. Mary Alice was her father's sister, and one day Aunt Mary Alice disappeared. No one ever discovered what happened, where she went. This mystery became the seed of Susan's last work.

Many of us were aware that Susan was circulating this manuscript at the time of her death. We had read and worked with her on many of the poems and consulted on the manuscript's arrangement. Thanks to Barbara Hagerty for knowing to search for the manuscript. Thanks to Frances Pearce for knowing how to find it. Thanks to Susan's many friends for knowing that the manuscript must be brought to Susan's readers. We expect Susan would have thanked so many others— *you know who you are*. Extra special thanks to Kevin Watson and Press 53 for publishing her final work. Proceeds will be donated to the poetry societies of North and South Carolina.

Tributes

The following tributes come to us from the baker's dozen of poets who helped shepherd this manuscript into the world. The italicized quotes between tributes come from Susan's poems.

Fringed and fleeting, such remnants,
though the world is full of them.

My sister had a family secret that haunted her
until she placed it on paper, spun into a mist of poetry.
Today, this cluster of poems weaves mysteries
of our Aunt Mary Alice's unsettled life. Some of
Susan's poems challenge the reader to search
for clues concerning her namesake and her long-dead aunt.

—*Janice Laughter Sullivan, sister*

Filled with lyric intensity and family mystery, these poems explore Susan Laughter Meyers's namesake aunt, a complex woman who struggled with mental illness. As if to refute the editor who once told Meyers that her "problem" was that her childhood was "too happy," these poems probe the depth of family dynamics, loss, and the desire for answers and understanding. The poems speculate and argue but provide no answers. Susan wrote poetry the way she lived her life, with intention and attention. This collection will leave you certain that *Something bold / has come & gone. Absence, like fire, / holds back nothing.*

—*Pat Riviere-Seel*

Emily Dickinson said, "Nature is a Haunted House—but Art—a House that tries to be haunted." These words haunt me as I read this collection. There is a haunting here by both the subject, Mary Alice, and by her not-so-obvious namesake, the late Susan Laughter Meyers. This is particularly evident in the poems

Tributes

"Hearsay" and "Mary Alice Alarm," which are haunted by the letters in the poet's and the subject's names, respectively. Both women, one I held dear and one I never knew, are lost to us in life, yet dwell on in these well-crafted poems.

—*Susan Finch Stevens*

In this delicate rendering of madness, Susan Laughter Meyers explores sorrow's *long, fading whistle*. With deftness, the poet draws her own *croquis of facts* spilling out her yearning for a complete portrait of loss. Language at times sane, nature-rich. At times a stutter of lost words. Perplexity laid open, an unsolvable tractate, skillfully explored, *An apron / with strings that keep coming untied.*

—*Libby Bernardin*

*Enter through any window
if the bees will let you.*

Susan took poetry seriously. After earning her MFA from Queens University of Charlotte, she continued to take classes and read books on craft. In June 2011, Susan drafted "Left by the River, Her Handbag and Shoes" (now titled "By the River") for an assignment in a poetry class led by Carol Ann Davis. I was in the class too and that's when Susan first told me about her aunt. She continued to explore questions about her aunt's fate by writing the poems that are contained in this stunning collection. Susan served as mentor to many and is deeply missed.

—*Frances J. Pearce*

Traditionally, Susan sat at the foot of Richard Garcia's Long Table. And there, she set for me the standard for poetic behavior: Humility, Hard Work, Dedication, Competence, Integrity, Generosity. At our last meeting together, she was trying out a new poetic form—so, I should add Innovation

Tributes

and Determination to her list of virtues. And, over the years, I never heard her speak ill of anyone, though I did notice, on occasion, a slight compression of her lips.

—Helen Brandenburg

Susan Laughter Meyers was a poet of rigor, scrupulosity, economy, measure, generosity, and grace. The consummate observer, she was also a poet of passion, often bringing back ecstatic dispatches from the natural world. Writing, burnishing, and sharing poetry were Susan's lifeblood and whole currency. For Susan—both in work and in life—the practice of poetry was sacred and special and, at the same time, radically ordinary.

—Barbara Hagerty

*Journey on past the farthest star,
out beyond honey & home.*

It's not often one can use accolades that are polar opposites to describe a friend, but genteel-strong, diligent-easygoing, leader-cheerleader all fit Susan Laughter Meyers. If you knew her and had lost your direction, whether in life or in writing, these constant and coalescing qualities helped you find your way. Read the words living on these pages, balanced with care, one upon another, like a cairn marking the path. Note the grace and gumption, the peaceful and the persevering, the exact and the yielding, vibrating like one single magnetic needle, freely suspended, that will lead you to your true north.

—Linda Annas Ferguson

For close to twenty years Susan Laughter Meyers guided Senior Thesis students at Charleston County School of the Arts. Susan met with them in the darkening library, took them for coffee, lent them books of poetry, and in general, loved them. She was my mentor too. I received encouraging notes about my work

Tributes

with students and gentle prodding to tend to my own poetry. If I was Mama to these students, Susan was our angel, watching over us all, giving us an invisible nudge to do more, think deeper, and always, impart the truth.

—*Rene Miles*

What we think about now is how reading Susan's poems have always taught us how to write our own poems. This final work, wrought from her study and skills and imagination, is richer, more complex, more meaningful than we thought to find— the newest poems, our latest gift from our beloved Susan, poems we will learn from.

—*Carol Peters*

Sitting here on the steps, I watch
for hummingbirds and the first sign of a tanager.

One of the last days I worked on Susan's books in the house she and Blue shared, we were packing the car and left the front door ajar. As I stood alone in the hallway a bird flew in, headed directly to her office, flew around the ceiling twice, and exited as it had entered. I chose to believe it was Susan's spirit coming to see the shifting of books from shelf to box to new hands, and when she didn't linger, chose to believe she said, "Good job. Thank you," to us all, in her always encouraging, gracious way.

—*Mary Harris*

Thank you to Kevin Watson and Press 53, for publishing Susan's final collection of poetry. Her sudden passing left us all shocked and saddened, but these new poems are a balm to heal our broken hearts. Susan Laughter Meyers was first and foremost a poet of precision. She carved each line like a sculptor, and the specific image details that fill her work bring the natural world to life before our eyes. With each and every poem we

Tributes

share in her delight. Always generous with literary advice and deep heartfelt wisdom, Susan left these poems as her final gift.

—*Marjory Wentworth, South Carolina Poet Laureate*

A spring blue-black night on the shoulder of a live-oak-lined Edisto back road, a Carole King CD in the player, five women harmonizing on the chorus of "Natural Woman," loud enough to compete with the peepers and raise the moon out of the sea. It was magical, and there was considerable LAUGHTER. Susan Laughter Meyers was with us—a natural, our lifeblood. In *Self-Portrait in the River of Déjà Vu* she is with us still.

—*Deborah Lawson Scott*

> *What else to shout out the window*
> *across the feathered fields but*
> *yes, open the sky—*

Foreword

To linger in this posthumous collection of poems by Susan Laughter Meyers is to be haunted by foreboding. Lines I discover and admire change, reread in the circumstance of the poet's recent passing. What doesn't read *about* her death? Even the most innocent expression of desire appears tinged: when a bird leaves a scene, there goes the future; when the river flows on, time does too; when the end of the poem approaches, we know we'll be separated, Susan just a little ways downstream, but no longer with us.

Such sadness, of course, presents a confounding metaphysical paradox: how can the poet's absence change the poem? Not everyone knew the poet, a fact that surely matters. Is the poem changed for everyone? (And maybe you already agree with some of the great literary thinkers, who argue that we never could know the poet, and never do . . .) Still, we have these stunning poems, these last words, their meanings seemingly different. How can the poem be changed by what I know and feel *before I read*? I leave that conundrum to you, dear reader, and to whatever you believe.

Because these are poems to know, to read and reread, art-acts to celebrate. These are poems ecstatic with potent images (or maybe potent with ecstasy): an aunt's disappearance, the shoes of a madwoman, a postcard from Paris, self-portraits of various denominations, summers of high skies and beginnings, last lines readying us for the beyond as "the ink is starting to fade . . ." Susan Laughter Meyers's poems were always a *textural* product, by which I mean to invoke both text and textile, but here her interest in surfaces and the sonic tapestry the language knits and purls (think Frost, think Moore), seems to have advanced. There's so much formal play here—couplets abounding, caesura and white space abuzz—as though the poet were holding each poem in her hands, sharing a discovery, what she made in the world and wants us to have too. This new, final *Self-Portrait* . . . has the heft of artifact, a collection of song-things.

Foreword

In the customary, we forget: life's repetitions dumb our sensibilities. Yes, the loss of a dear one serves to loosen the increasing fixity of habit, and in the funereal we hear the future echoing already. But art helps too, as it always has and will, and Susan's fine final poems help a lot. Although maybe it would offer a smidge more comfort, dear reader, to pass by with a smile each sad moment in this collection, trusting that the poet herself would be smiling (dear Susan!) to find us here.

We miss you, Susan. Thanks for the poems.

—Alan Michael Parker

I.

*until a name
and all its connotation are the same*

—Elizabeth Bishop

For All Anyone Knows

The wasps congregating on the wind chimes, late August,
mistook them for a cathedral.

Aunt M., missing for years, didn't drown herself in the river.
My brother, right about her husband after all.

Who says our brief lives aren't mere wishes?
So much for heat, for particle and wave.

The last one tagged "It" still roams the neighborhood
calling, *Where are you? I give up.*

Aunt M.'s name could have been a pass-along plant.
It ended up with me.

The ocean view from the dunes no one is allowed to climb,
a postcard never sent.

Wish you were here. Code for: *I'm glad you're not.* Code for:
Help, please, help.

Code for: *Is only one of us okay?*

Stitchery & the Child

In the air a smell of fruit, maybe peaches.
This is not the day of the funeral

for anyone the family knows, nor a holiday.
Not even Sunday, so there's no rest.

An aunt who rarely comes to town
sits and works on her Swedish weaving

in a den quiet enough to hear a wasp
worry the screen at the open window.

Another hand towel with stair-step stitches
the child touches and calls *pretty,* satin

floss climbing nowhere and back
like the child's monkey bars

that coax her to cross—hanging hand
over hand. Sometimes she falls.

A breeze drifts in from the backyard
and the aunt starts to rock, the grass

near the fence sweet and tender.
Grazing there, two small rabbits.

Finding Her Huck Embroidery Folded in a Drawer

That day I was a child
with an aunt who balanced

my invisible name—a crock
atop her head.

Another day it tumbled
& cracked to pieces.

~

I know the answer, unbreakable.
Ask me again,

I don't know half the answer.
No one does, no one did. No one

answer. What made us think
there was one question?

~

My mind is a river
she is lost in, even now.

I would bury her if I could
but she says no. Listen,

her dead self
still rides these currents.

(Now Again) I Am Calling Out

This time I wonder what you needed
to be cured of—and why the cure never came.
I think of you when the sun is fading
or when I see a woman in a fitted jacket
that gapes between horn-bone buttons.
Your body took pleasure

in the press against its clothes. Your face,
that round perplexity of mostly forehead,
laid itself open. There are some
who wear a shield between their face
and the world. Not you,
who clenched your mouth closed

with deliberation, like shutting the door
to your room. When you opened it to talk,
what loud hesitation and sputtering. Off
to an uncertain start, as if you were of two minds.
A rock in a brook has the same effect,
making the water choose which path.

Your mouth slipped that thin boat of lips
into a deep smile even while you were searching
for words. To speak was to click on the radio
whose volume was already turned up.
Here I am. To speak, even opaquely—
there we go—was to claim a space.

Sometimes to speak was to laugh,
the storm of it rising without warning.
The thin boat of lips, a canoe working the wind.
How your laugh, the thrill of it, turned you over
into rocking. I thought you'd capsize,
and a time or two you did.

on good days you would

                    on good days
you would wear spectator pumps
& matching handbag on your arm
dab at pursed lips with a napkin
smile back (or first) you would
speak (breathless) words that fit
though a few too loud you would
turn on a spigot of laughter

                        you would
embrace your (ample) misgivings
head high like blades of tall grass
lie down in a wet field of clover
polish two old stones you would
polish prayer stones for kneeling
wring your hands at the clouds
you would let loose your longing
walk but not into the rising river

Namesake

One day you walked away
and left "Alice"
       for me to carry,
your shoes and purse laid out by the river
where the cab driver last saw you.

      What did you mean
that time when I was seven?
Cover your mouth, you said but you were the one
contagious, your laugh
           the next thing to crying.

They couldn't cure you,
couldn't stop the weeping—*carrying on,*
Mother called it,
any woman who'd let loose that way.

              As for the children,
we weren't laughing with you,
that high forehead sunk into a hat,
my father's
      youngest sister, top wound up, helpless,
with my favorite name.

Your voice I remember. Fluttery, loud.
A fishing line
      unreeled.
You, the reason for letters and family
quarrels, the silence that followed.
              "Mary Alice,"
once sweet to my father's lips. Now, no more
than one more
        missing.

Under the Waning Moon

There are days you barely speak,
thoughts bogged deep
in pluff mud: what lies
       sunken,
               a grave of regret.
Wolves roam your fears at night.
Whatever you can't abide
breeds in you
       sullenness.
               Night after night
combing the fog of your troubled
sleep, red wolves.
Wild, gracile & dolorous.

Other days you wrap both arms
around yourself to contain the green,
aiming
       to count each blade of it.
Thick, the grasses & reeds—
a whole landscape teeming.
You want to swim
             the creek of you.
To float, a limber leaf. To feel
the current's nudge, that kissable
swell of minnows
       as they flee.

Stars-on-the-River Tanka

why the nieces hide
come old fluster & windstorm
enter a swirled skirt
voice raised an octave shaking
her voice walking a tightrope

other times she's still
born with a merry-mouth name
my father's last name
help can't somebody help please
her rumpled white handkerchief

let's say she craves sweets
I think she'd like marmalade
that clear slick amber
spooned & smeared on buttered toast
thick with rind to hunger through

her forehead is wide
her forehead spans high sky high
in-out check into
tilting at the edge so close
sanitarium again

everywhere she weeps
she tells it to the river
that quick suck-in breath
her laugh a bale of loose hay
any minute she could fall

twigs caught in currents
all is mud mud after rain
stars on the river
hole worn through my father's heart
something like a drowning hole

Beast with no name

with no shadow, the one
that bushwhacks tomorrow

& devours the green rows
tended in the mind's garden.

My father's family fed it
tobacco worms & the youngest.

She, she. . . they didn't like
to talk about it, though

always her in the letters
& the house in Ringwood,

a house under vines.
Her laugh matched the murder

of crows quarreling nearby.
A person could die

laughing. Imagine the seeds
she watered with weeping.

Obbligato: Her Faithless Muse

She could have been a glass harmonicist
in a rain forest of quick, bright birds.

They would hold like deep reverberations.
They would hum from her clavicle.

Her one gift, a circle of ringing—
long feathered and ethereal.

Could have been, a sour lingering.
What but slim fingertips (trembled

by hitch) diminished her song
to rough-weathered half notes?

To orchids, bromeliads. That glad-
edged serenade—gone brickle-mad.

She Could Have Been a Planter Woman

sweetbitter unmanageable creature who steals in
with the moon's half-shuttered light on her face,

who has spun the lids of the glittering quart jars
now tight-sealed and burgundy with beets,

who has tilled (not without cursing) each row
of zipper peas and chopped (unsmiling)

the careless weeds near the front-acre ditch
where the blackberry briars cross-stitch

over the pitiless snakes, unapologetic
and tangled in the pleasure of the smallest secret—

how she warms each threshold, that one and this,
distracting blowsy creature come from the day's

munificence, both hands loose-wristed in hip pockets,
lips stung by refusal, heart intractably free

The Art of Beginning

first you sketch   what on another day would be
erased   your dead father's eyes   you remember
from that year   quick the thumbnail   a reminder
like a five-o'clock alarm   time (later) to fill in
the hair   on anyone's head   your youngest aunt
who by now would be gone   untraceable
her purse & shoes lined up by the river   not wet
despite the storm   a private detective said   bank on it
the husband you barely knew   his white-haired mother
it's all so   undelineated   this croquis of facts
& what was he like   why wasn't he liked
there was a time   you could ask an older cousin
your sister six then (that small figure)   begged to go
on the honeymoon   (the past a pale wash)
with the favorite from the farm   Aunt Estelle
& her husband   not the one she's buried beside
sweet pentimento   that would be Joe

Ringwood

Halifax County, NC

Enter through any window
if the bees will let you in.

The dry slatted wood smells
of summers before you were born.

Before your grandmother
swaddled your father in cotton

and fanned the cradle to quiet him,
before blackberries purpled

his thumbs and briars tattooed
his wrists ankles and shins.

Dust clouds the window panes,
spider webs are hard to read.

This is the doorway your father
walked through when he first

stepped out into the world. North
south east and west, still the same.

The rest of what you came for
is gone, but the oak and house

with its Virginia creeper greening
up one side. In the sills, dead bees

lie on their backs. Over hills
of them the live ones crawl.

The Last Summer with Her Sisters: What to Wear

At Estelle's I have my own bedroom,
plus this spare room—a sink
& windows all around. Ironing board,
guineas to feed. I should be happy.

Mornings oscillate like a fan.
The foolhardy squirrels leap through air.
Why do I sit here by the window, dusting
the sill with one finger?

Estelle promised she'd teach me to drive,
but when I get behind the wheel
the hood looks like a boulder
in the road—& where would I go?

By the fencepost, a bluebird
on its back—its pointy little beak
half-open, never again to snap up a bug
with feet paddling air. Dead, dead.

Milton is coming & I'm all nerves.
What to wear. The beige outfit
from the nieces? or the print dress?
I hate deciding. Estelle will know.

Dress of Flame & Upside-Down Bird

They climb onto the walls
& dresses—long, flowing dresses.
She touches each syllable with her eyes,
confessing them one by one.

They refuse to line up
in obedience. How they tumble
in disarray, clicking
their consonants like glass beads.

Here's the logic: upside-down
bird = any-side-up fugue of falling.
Niagras cascading
the walls & dresses, etched on skin.

Abundant as dandelions, careless
when ripe & the wind blows. Some days
elegies loose as the bark of the river
birch. They flutter like prayer flags.

Why are the walls & faces rising
all ashimmer?
Innuendoes fly from them slantwise
& drift from lips to fingertips.

Untongued, she says inside her mouth
after she's lit by morning. She sits
& takes inside her body all the shaped
flames until she is a book of them.

The Last Summer with Her Sisters: A Day of Barking

When the spaniels, penned up,
hear the deer hounds running loose
in the countryside, nothing appeases them.
A day of barking & I come undone.

It punctuates the air, a cadence
& howl that hurts my ears.
How to hush this racket
and spawn it into dog song.

We picked butterbeans soon after dawn.
Still the heat got to me.
Now I'm shelling them while Estelle
drives to town. I don't even eat beans.

The biggest hen is eyeing me,
cocking her head from side to side
& blinking. I wish she liked me.
That fixed stare. *Don't touch my egg.*

I cut my thumb peeling a tomato.
Even Milton says I'm no good
in the kitchen. Mama used to say
I whine better than anything else.

Mary Alice Alarm

Mama, call me
a lame liar.
Rail me.

Yell, rile, clear
my crime.
I'll marry
my lyric aria.

I am a relic.
Mercy, mercy,
a clay miracle.

[Let's say you forgot me]

Let's say you forgot me—
no, not forgot: were unable to reach,
one of us out of the country,
say, me this time
writing in France. I put down line
after line, shapes anyone could make
something out of,
black ink on cream paper, waiting for you
to call. Your phone, my phone,
somebody's phone isn't working.
My thoughts are growing remote,
and the words come to me
in a language I can't translate.
Weeks pass, as weeks will do.
My handwriting becomes illegible
and the ink is starting to fade.

II.

*Dearest, I feel certain
that I am going mad again.*

—Virginia Woolf

Aunt Mary Alice Teaches Me to Tat

If I could see where the shuttle goes,
I could follow. I can't see. She holds it
in her right hand. Left handed,
like my grandmother on my mother's side,
I sit across from her, knee to knee.
Her eyes, on the shuttle, are lost to me.

I am almost ten, tapping one foot.
Her face is a broad explanation, her mouth
a rapt O. Sometimes she leans so close
I can feel her breath warm on my face.
With a ring of thread lacing her fingers,
she pulls the shuttle through and tugs.

The skein in my fingers is off-white
and unwinding, the ball of it falling
to the floor. Her loud laugh unthreads
any thought that she is well. She could break
again at any moment, her raspy voice
bearing down on me. A fly crawls on the arm

of her chair. A summer fly—that slow,
dazzling stutter my mother always tries
to keep out of the house. What to make of it
when Aunt Mary Alice flinches, as if the devil
himself has sat down beside her. She slides
a knot to her left thumb and index finger.

I slide a tangle. Soon she has a double stitch,
and I have nothing. She is abuzz, moving on
to double stitch and picot, a ring of them.
Not for me, this finger work! She sings
her fancy song of double stitch and picot.
My lesson, a snarl of string untatted.

Mary Alice Tanka

it's hot I am three
she stands beside someone's car
a back door open
her hair is brown wavy curled
my beautiful youngest aunt

for now there's laughter
she's wearing her shirtwaist dress
sand on my bare feet
my arms wrap around her legs
she looks just like my father

she talks loud loud loud
she talks when she's inhaling
there's wind in her voice
where are Milton his mother
they're in a house in Richmond

her face is open
her face is open water
no white caps at sea
she crashes high and low tides
months spent at Aunt Estelle's house

there are long letters
letters about what to do
what to do for her
the siblings write and argue
Uncle Milton's fault they think

someone make it right
in and out of asylums
weeping and wailing
she carries a purse and gloves
she wears her felt hat and veil

her Swedish weaving
she does huck embroidery
pale finger towels
she crochets long dresser scarves
and fancy round white doilies

I have one of them
I too crocheted a doily
which is hers which mine
her cross stitch on beige monk cloth
shiny x's untwisted

I lost her last name
now I've found it carraway
that's her married name
it will carry her away
my mary alice *[last name]*

drowned hair of women
whose hair has the river drowned
hair of drowned women
birdsong in the empty woods
leaves torn from a tree its roots

birdsong that has stopped
echoes of birdsong still here
a wren's tea kettle
a body turning away
a log rolling in currents

everywhere she weeps
she walks down near the river
each step each deep breath
clay pots are turned and broken
by the windstorm blowing in

If Not Birds Dodging Loneliness

The bluest ones in an open sky
fan reveries with their wings.
Dream time, that's what they inhabit—
fabulous as the past and its dingy veils

I wore in a favorite childhood game:
dress-up with the girl whose father
ran a funeral home. The newest shrouds
had no holes to trip us, one a princess

the other a bride. The least breeze
and the shroud would ripple, barely
kissing the skin. Wasn't that a dalliance
to wish for? On days when birds soar

toward light, when they tip and wheel
and turn until they silhouette,
you'd think they're being chased.
Or if not birds dodging loneliness,

then memories loosed into view.
Like the ones of a blindfolded
child with stick or pin-and-tail in hand,
steering toward a prize, when to win

the game is to break something
or make something whole again.
Fringed and fleeting, such remnants,
though the world is full of them.

There are moments in my life
when gravitating *toward* feels the same
as ducking *from*. Moments when,
for recompense, I look back. Or up.

Abstractionists & Love: The Art of Forgetting

1. *Phenomena Prevailing Wind*

Up this high, good Jesus,
and without a prayer
to bank on.
Send me east, Lord,

and shoulder me up
with bright intention.
Lift the day, or coming night,
with your sigh or littlest finger.

2. *Fine and Mellow*

Impossible to ignore,
memory's ciphers, faint
as a line of trees
scribbled in fog
that rides the colorless sky,
not quite indelible,
not quite erased.

3. *Deep Water*

At first no one wants to go there.
Besides, how to jump from a mast
angled in uncertainty, the constant rocking
red as a winter sunset. Besides,
how to sink. One glance up
and who wouldn't climb to the top
if only to look back.

This blank tomorrow a sail pulling you somewhere
you've never been. To drift is to decide
not to decide, and you have decided to drift
in cubic blue, this block of it,
length times width times depth, squared
to the volume of something you've lost measure of.
That's the terrible swell, that's how deep.

4. *Eye of Chimu*

When evening unfolds itself,
boxes of brown longing
tumble one over the other—
torn open and falling
into this shy relief:

something is left standing   cantilevered
something is left inside   half hidden
what the merciless day has cracked open.

5. *One River*

She gives me dancing, a rhythm of legs
dangling in mystery, the right one
(or second from the right) leviathan blue
and a left one (any left one)
redder than the breast of a bream.
This, at midnight when she slow-dances me
past shadow and a reckoning of green
that repeats itself like a phonograph needle
stuttering its one syllable of love.

6. *Search*

The ladder climbs past smaller
and smaller windows, smoke
rolled into balls of worry.

Arrow or rooftop, no matter.
In the wind, as if speed-reading,
a book flips its own pages.

On which street were you born
or have the flames eaten
that good memory too?

The Last Summer with Her Sisters: Swedish Weaving

No wonder the mule looks so frazzled—
pulling a full tobacco drag
from the field to the shed. Back
& forth. Just watching makes me tired.

The work horse is as slow as the mule.
Sometimes George hoists a niece,
grinning, into the saddle
& leads the horse up & down the dirt road.

Today a man came to fell the loblollies
near the house. When the largest tree
hit the dirt, I thought God
was shaking me by my shoulders.

Nancy is here. She's teaching me
to do Swedish weaving. Her stitching
on the hand towels is neater
than mine. I keep pricking my finger.

Every poke of the needle, each tiny
stitch—one more reminder
that you are the chosen sister, Nancy.
Why am I all pucker, twists & stabs?

A Little Wildness

                                                 One more question.
In my crazy heart whom should I persuade (now again)
to embrace a little wildness, shagged as tendrils

of moss hanging in the live oak at the back door:
the banker with his strict accuracy,

the judge with his even handedness, the planter
& tiller, whose fields have inched past

their symmetry? Spilled sprigs & resurrection ferns.
Islands of lichens, rivers of bark.

Soon cicadas will shake late summer to its husks
& moss will swing sideways in wind.

The Last Summer with Her Sisters: Long Past Sunup

Last night, a noise out my window.
Maybe a raccoon, George says.
I heard whispers, I did. And then
I heard the family chanting my name.

At Sunday dinner Mae & Ed's
youngest girl coughed at the table.
As soon as I said, *Cover your mouth,*
I saw it. She was fixing to cry.

In the henhouse this morning I wrapped
my hand around the warmth & held
the weight of each egg a little longer,
pitying the hens I'd robbed.

Estelle says to ignore the dogs,
but the barking wears at my bones.
When I was ten, after Willie Bell died
I felt the same ache & tug.

Dark outside long past sunup.
Dark inside. Lying here in bed, I think
how small my life is. An apron
with strings that keep coming untied.

Hearsay

Unleash the harangue.

Telegrams, a thesaurus—useless.

Thermals are rhymeless,

gaunt & easterly.

Tarantulas & tattlers stammer.

Seam all leather hems, guess

the hunger. Tangle the lame laughs.

Are there sage mares at the gates?

Are there masterly sane men?

Argue Hamlet's glum,

the usual slugs & slathers—

my shame, urgent, unseemly.

An asylum, yes. Hurtless.

Tear my musher heart.

Sundog Sonnet

I know you, Scowling Angel, Angel of Broken Things.
I'm sorry I didn't adore you but complained bitterly instead.
Dog that never slept in our house, that chased cars—
dog that never roamed my childhood, gone. Years later,
over and over, the smoke of it. And God said the cars with shiny
hood ornaments will come to a stop in rows. Let sunlight slant
through the window and its translucent shade. Let a prism
follow the sun, the way a dog follows its master. A sundog.

Angel of Silence with sundog eyes, hold out your arms
and embrace the air, whose traffic has thinned to bare branches.
Not far from the river, native spider lilies droop, frostbitten
and obscenely transparent. This time of year goldfinches cling
to the thistle sock, and they flee. O my favorite stranger, call
the crows. The backyard is a pantry of suet and seed.

Late Summer

Is it the smell of fresh-cut grass
and sliced leaves,
plus the plea of some small bird
in the weeds and vines?
Crooked sticks woven
through the fence wire.
O the loud machinery of cicadas.
What else to shout out the window
across the feathered fields but
yes, open the sky—
Up with the roof!
Yes, open the sky
across the feathered fields but
what else to shout out the window?
O the loud machinery of cicadas.
Through the fence wire
crooked sticks woven
in the weeds and vines,
plus the plea of some small bird.
And sliced leaves.
Is it the smell of fresh-cut grass?

Why My Heart Has Renamed Itself Mercy

I've learned
to conjure dreams from a sprinkler.

Wolfberry
roves the thickets within me,

a nightjar
somewhere ruffling its song.

Forgive me?
I cling to the rungs of a ladder

I can't climb.
Only a stumble or two away.

Over my steeple,
and without a veil, the moon.

In the greenhouse
lives a fallen matador.

He, untamed,
reads my ceiling, star by star.

Sonata of Tomatoes

Sleepwalker bees balance on toes
inch by inch. Or some-
thing wished for like toes, while they test

the tilt of lilies. The state
of saw palmettos raveling at the seam.
With force the wind has smote

a little green. Serrated edges taste
like drifts of days spread on toast.
A violinist plays from a nearby moat.

Why My Heart Has Renamed Itself Shock Therapy

Father, tomato worms
climb the shadows inside me.

All my dreams
are half-chewed chewed somethings.

Tomorrows maybe.
They no longer long to wake me

with blossoms.
Dust devils twirl & take

my darlings.
Well, they take my everythings.

You know
I cannot live on the farm.

This place, though—
cold, rough, like my hands.

Easy to want
a day with or without little moons.

Harder, watching
a season eat the marrow away.

Anytime Soon, Fall

          On bad days
crows chant their calls
to you & only you:
I simply want to be dead.

It's not dying you desire
but to be done with it.
To quiet the tongue, fold
your furious hands.
          Once, bursting
into your husband's office,
a brother & sister by your side,
you keened in no key I know
winging north or south.

My father, that brother,
shaking his head, what will it take
to settle you.
          Not the Chickahominy
nor Chuckatuck Creek.
But to the James River
one morning you fly off.
          Wanting in. So little,
& so much, to ask. How
to get to the bottom of it,
to still the quiver.

          Wait,
anyone would say—
look up. See? Clouds, reshaped,
are parting.
          Shoes, tied together
by their laces & hanging
from a telephone wire,
will not, anytime soon, fall.

A mockingbird, same wire—
singing, that bird,
someone else's song.

Her Evening with Monet

The port shimmers & what lies below
no one will say. Where are the gulls?
Laughing gulls could match voice to light.
I am lost in the dichotomy of missing leaves.
Or is it the dread of leaving?
Weighted as six fat crayons, broken.
Strokes flung to sky. I am a felled tree floating.
Some say, *Catch a boat, stranger*—
or idle in safe harbor. But what good, advice
from those still treading?
Deep in the thick of it, another song,
faint but wearable. Again & again,
the water's refrain. I could lay my skin open
to the lull. Yet the debris.
A wall divides my city inside. Do not expect
to save me. Here I belong to bedlam.

The Last Summer with Her Sisters: A Dervish of Sand

Milton has asked me to marry him.
His mother would live with us.
Strong willed, that woman—the way
she glares at the two of us together.

Some summer days I wake up in winter.
The smallest squall pummels me.
Drifting, I'm certain of this:
I cannot predict my own weather.

My hands wring themselves.
Wind twists in circles
across empty fields. I could die
from rocking, no one to still me.

I wish it would rain, slantwise torrents
beating the roof & the oak by the porch,
pitting the dirt. If only
clouds would drop their weight.

In my ears this storm, a dervish of sand.
The guineas so loud, flocked
inside my head, trying to roost.
Such a fuss. Quick, get the broom.

Weave Such Days to a Whole

Suppose dried goldenrod hangs by the door
and the door is blue, propped open in autumn
with a half-bristled broom. Sunlight, slanting
through the window, breaks into pieces
on the floor. Something heavy is in the air,
though what could be simpler than flowers,
a window, a door in the face of morning?

sweet mother I cannot work the loom

There are days when sunlight is not enough,
all the little pieces, though dazzling and discrete,
can't turn the task aright; when the heart
is blue as a heavy door; when dead flowers
shed their seeds, and the broom—straw bent
and broken—has curled too far. Who can thread
the loom to weave such days to a whole?

Train Headed South

Long, like the night, the lonely car
(it could be red), coupled to the yearning car
coupled to the homesick car.
The hopeful and forgiving too.
And all the cars I cannot name or see.
Some surely bloom their graffiti
like giant tulips, fat, purple, and bruised.
Under the laws of trains, the whistle sounds
the indecipherable code
all passersby have tried to crack
since the coming and going of trains.
Something about what's ahead
and what's behind. Something about
what never was and never will be.
The last one startled me, the whistle
out my bedroom window,
though I felt the clacking coming.
I see the engine light.
The ground shakes under me.
Sorrow is a long, fading whistle.
Once gone, all that is left:
a trace of quiet, time
to regard what's missing.
Whatever feared I still fear. I know, too,
the train—its wheels (the greased connectors),
those hard, heavy bearers of weight—
will roll over me, again and again.

Lately She Falls to Dreaming

The day's clarity, its sky in the pond,
is lost to her. Propitious, the night
with its faint trails
                    crossing.
Through the dry grasses
of moonlight, field mice skitter.
The owl comes on silent wings.
                          Unstoppable,
some things. Words
she has memorized—his, rubbed
and worn smooth, a flood of them.

Those quick smudges, the moths
at her window screen tapping in code.
Who can decipher the pulse?
                          Rudderless
and veiled, her weather. The spell
she's under: a wash of hunger.
A rasp. The riffling wind.

Her One and Only

beautiful he
wears my old love

like a necklace
someone dropped

on a path
the river path to town

and he
unfaltering

he finding it broken
has restrung

every bead
even the chipped yellow one

First Sign of Bad Weather

1. *The Young Sailor*

He occupies the chair
as if it were rigging
       he has climbed,

an eye and a leathered
ear cocked
for the first sign
       of bad weather.

2. *Icarus*

In the next-to-the-last dream
(the cerulean one)

he swims among stars—

gathering speed,
rapt and aglow.

3. *Sorrows of the King*

Not the plucked guitar,
its empathetic notes.

Not the dark-haired woman
whirling on small feet.

Not prayers rising
from fingerlike wings.

Nor the single petals loosed
into the season,

a stir of them, not the ladder
of air, the self reflected—

nor even the flowers,
six yellow blossoms, floating.

Burial Notes

you can take nothing out

This is the night I am stripped
down to me, only moonlight
moored to my body,
the sound of water falling
comes one note at a time,
floating above me.
This is the night the air is not mine,
the breeze is not mine,
the dark does not enter my eyes
nor does the light—
the smell of mown grass
for someone else,
the news of the latest war
not my news.
The vines are cut.
Finches, having brightened
and flown north for nesting,
will not return this season.

Detective Notes
1/28/65

- ✓ 9 to 11:25am @house:
  husbnd left/came bk—twice
  (jittery, rushd);
    blinds closed, car parkd on st.

- ✓ talkd w/ cabbie again:
  yes to river address;
  she pd in cash.
    wore coat, dress & heels

- ✓ trip to Williamsburg:
  Eastern State Hospitl—aka "Public Hospitl
  for Persons of Insane & Disorderd Minds"
    committed there 4x (poor woman!)

- call wife's nephw Gene (SH1-1926)
  for scoop on husbnd;
  employd @same co.,
    H.M. Furniture (FL9-9171)

- call other contcts:
  start w/ oldest bros. James/Edgar;
  sis. Estelle: opinion of husbnd?
    divorce ever mentioned?

- ck w/ neighbrs:
  anything odd—argumnts,
  drinking, fightng?
    hrs. of coming & going?

- which paving co. for drivewy repair?
  contct sales rep & crew supervsr:
  conditn of old drivewy?
    date of excavatn?

Farewell Meditation

Crows say what they know.
Cousins know things they don't say.
Cows mull over the mundane,
munching sweet, translucent grass.

Cousins hunch old knowings.
Cows jump bales & moons.
Crows, in rain, wing
to a mull of wet, elusive marsh.

Cows chew good, thick hearsay.
Crows fling days unseamed.
Cousins, bunched & waning, hum
a spell of clouds that, too, shall pass.

I Open the Door

I open the door to my shadow,
my smallness turning inside out
and folding.
   It no longer gives
or takes orders. I open the door.
Windows cannot hold me

and my long petition,
the unstoppable river
born of all the words
     I've embraced
since thin boned
and squirming in the pew.

    One day
I'll open windows too,
though the one facing north
has been painted blue
     and shut,
overlooking a hill
I climb twice daily.

If only they could save me.
Long ago I promised myself.
Have the strictest
    of my old lessons
turned their backs on me
and the wild creatures trailing me?

A shame, not to open the door.
I will not close it from old habit,
even when the wind
    bullies through.
Nor will I close it to shivers
or threats of big-fisted enemies.

Opening, I place there a door stop
in the shape of a bell whose tongue
looses all my bitter
     and better selves.

III.

all things swept sole away
this – is immensity –

—Emily Dickinson

Anniversary Song

A door, it's only a door
of old wood. Paint peels

in streaks of turquoise
coppered by sunlight.

The top brace (one end
rot-chewed) shoulders

wide boards, all four.
No latch, a knotted rope

worming through the key-
hole half-hitches a nail.

Anointed Yet Badly Blessed

the doorkeeper's feet are seven armlengths long,
the mythweaver's thumb breaks the bowl.

One wears grace, the other black roses.
Which one crowns the sandaled winter with wings,

which is quick to gather a throat of violets
and burn the evening's loose-woven garlands?

After sleep twists, midair, dropping to earth—
sparrows will come unwilling and dead.

O beautiful shiver of leaves near the bees
weeping and fragrant with poverty.

O holy lamb lethargic with otherworldliness,
remember the face of your absent mother.

The night spangled with piercing white stars
has answered few punishing questions.

Come dawn, the weaver will swear an oath of honey,
the doorkeeper will not be persuaded.

You Offer Apology

but I to you of a white goat
say nothing till barbed

by the fence
that defines this withering.

No climb can snatch
what rises beyond reach.

You I forgive,
sorry or not.

Bearded by what falsehood,
nudged by whose hunger

under
which bridge?

Don't answer that. All I ask
is a creek bed of stones.

Anatomy of a Drowning

    James River

Her body a flight   of arms, their abduction.
A stitch   drops from the mind's basketweave.
Her quivered knees   & caudal mockeries
sucked,   unsaving her. Cursive, that path.

How did she get to this   sorrow house hiding
the gist of it?   Behind silt curtains & brack.
She once outspent   fallow fields—
her body   a flight of arms, their abduction.

Who can know what paled   the greening
or why? A long story   to plot the end of,
the runnel   to her, a glove of fingers fanned.
A stitch drops from the mind's   basketweave

& leaves a foxed hole   for the day moon.
For those left   the west wind hums, it hums
a gale. The grace of hands risen,   her feet—
her quivered   knees & caudal mockeries.

A bird whistles metallic, the after-air   stilled
or half stilled.   Perpetual blaming. A flight
of dropped   stitches, the body's affections
sucked, unsaving her.   Cursive, that path.

Her Purse Is a Room for Sleeping

Her voice, the gift of it, a sky of starlings.
Her handkerchief, an unplowed acre.
Her shoes on the riverbank, a blue purling.

Winter trees minus leaves & someone's darling
is gone. Call it a bottomless ache—or
her voice, the shift of it, a sky of starlings.

Say she caught a cab & left—such sorrowing—
or drowned & now she's the town's newsmaker.
Shoes on the riverbank, a blue purling.

Breath, I know, is only a borrowing,
but why would she beg the current to take her?
Her voice, the rift of it, a sky of starlings.

Is her chestnut hair nested & swirling?
All's erased. No need for the undertaker.
Shoes on the riverbank cast a blue purling.

Morning knells—a soughing & arcing,
a skirl of birds too buoyant to wake her.
Her voice, the drift of it, a sky of starlings.
Two shoes on the riverbank, blue unpurling.

Spirits on the river

    not for you to tell Virginia   stones
to tumble over   stones to batter knees
        rimmed light   widening
                      water
of torn sky   no east from west   up from down
    rain-soaked swell
pocketed stones   heavy chest Ophelia
            glint & glimmer
there's rue   *for you*
    the current   nothing really
            if it doesn't trundle you
        tug   have mercy   ghosts drum
the body Virginia   threads of minnows
                    transparent
coursing your fingers   your hair
        coursing between your legs
                  the river
yields   secrets Ophelia   each blue one
                bartered for you
      and you   and   and

The Blue of What Remains

    after Charles Wright

Blue is for tenderness, the proximate, the bent note;
The dragonfly's thorax, that blue, pearl of moon;
Long shadow, the blue of wistfulness;
The blue of landscapes, their blue slopes;
The sacred blue of birth;
Imaginative blue, the blue of breath;
The dotted blue, telling who gives and who receives;
The blue of bluebottles, two twigs of a devilwood;
The blue of what remains;
Blue of juniper, blue of moss;
The blue of vessels; the blue below the lids;
The blue of inkwells, their transparent skin;
Chicory blue, sweet salad;
The blue of glacier, the wind, the bridge back.

[Lately when sorrows come]

Lately when sorrows come—fast, without warning—
whipping their wings down the sky,
I know to let them.
Not inviting them, but allowing each
with a deep breath as if inhaling a wish I can't undo.

Some days the sky is so full of sorrows
they could be mistaken for shadows of unnamed
gods flapping the air with their loose black sleeves:
the god of head-on collisions,
the god of amputated limbs,
the god of I'll-dress-you-in-mourning.

Is the buzz in the August trees,
that pulsing husk of repetition, an omen?
I hear it build to a final shaking. I hear it build
louder and louder, then nothing.
Like a long, picaresque novel that's suddenly over.
Like the last inning of kickball until the rain.

What falls from the sky is not always rain
or any kind of weather. Call it precipitous.
I'm fooling myself, of course. Wearing sorrow
is nothing like skin shedding water.
It's more like the weight of a cloak of crows.

And yet the sun still shines on the honey locust
arching its fringe over grass. Lit, too,
the pasture and its barbwire strung from post
to leaning post. See how the stump by the road
is rotting and how the small yellow leaves, twirling,
catch light on their way to the ground.

The Body

    after Dana Levin

On the lowest limb of the pine a hawk
    plucks feathers from a cardinal.

Brilliant, the body pinned by talons.
    Do you feel the pull? Lightly, light

as a feather the feathers fall and turn
    in summer's long light. Some land

on scattered pine needles. Are you glad
    not to miss this moment's air

raining its sad diagonals?
    The hawk lowers his head again

and raises it, again and again
    in the rhythm of a woman stitching closed

the end of a pillow
    she has just stuffed with down,

a woman who draws her arm wide
    from the body, out and back.

Above the wound of red the hawk's breast
    is creamy, his shoulders a dull madder,

though you might say they're bright
    compared to pine needles. Occasionally

the hawk turns his head as if to see
    who's watching. More feathers fall.

Why are you afraid, standing at the window
    with a plate of glass between you

and the body coming undone
    on this hot July afternoon?

Postcard from Paris, a Deciphering

It could be from her. She's alive?
Could not good enough.

That day her shoes and purse
there by the river. The taxi driver

said she was the one. The postcard says,
Here I am—Paris! Or, *Her I am*?

The postcard, unsigned. Just like her
to delete herself.

Handwriting, like hers. And not.
You could get lost in the *a*'s, loose

and open, those empty sacks.
Was she in a rush, though

who ever knew her to hurry?
I read it backwards and upside down.

Welcome. . . or, *We'll come.*
White, my moon. . . or, *Write me soon.*

A cryptic, *To do or know, want. . .*
or, *The door knob, wait.*

Wish you. . . or maybe, *Miss you.*
Paradise—am I here?

Self-Portrait as a Small Journey

I am a rowboat
nudged by minnows.

A skiff needled
through the slender pass.

Canoe oared
between rocks, behind me

a drift of light that scatters
unstitched flames.

Each morning I tilt
like a pot of looseleaf tea.

When wind ruffles clouds
& steeples waves,

it unperplexes me like honey.
Wind is not the gist of me.

Should I dream
of the horse latitudes

& ferry the ghosts
of seven red angels?

Refuse to yield
to the dirge of sunset?

Daily I map the sky.
Cousin to mishap, step-

child of the open sea.

Anatomy of a Supposed Life Undrowned

Last night she came back   to her brothers & sisters
(dead now),   came back distal   to her own story,
its insinuations   & her hair was dry. I think Aunt Estelle
was right about the postcard   from Paris

& I think my brother   was wrong about the old
driveway dug up   & newly paved. Her hair
wavy   & dry. A bruise yellowed her left wrist.
Last night she came back   to her brothers & sisters,

shoulders (still too sagged to cry on)   superior
to elbows   abducted in prayer. She was that calm,
standing & swaying.   She did sway. Her voice
(dead now)   came back distal   to her own story:

gapped   as if clotted with branches   & wet leaves.
The past   dorsal & deep to her. A proximal smile.
Her throat swam the river   of *déjà vu*,   stuttered
its insinuations & her hair   was dry. I think Aunt Estelle

saved the Manila envelope   she showed me once,
with all the names   & dates. The handwriting looped
& slanted.   If not so, she willed it,   proof she
was right   about the postcard from Paris.

Not one single further sorrow

here, where this morning the three horses nuzzled
at the fence near the gravel road,
their chestnut heads and necks glistening—

here, where I could forget sorrow
and how the young woman from class that summer
gave up on herself, and the news spread quickly,

or, if not a forgetting, a diminishment—the way the horizon
across the field of grasses and bachelor's buttons
softens its line to a fringe of blossoms and stems.

Rain

Come again another day.

Let today be that other day. Unleash.
May the saw palmettos clatter, the tea olive leaves
dip and tip their oily sheen. Torrent. Bead
and slicken my skin, drench me. Not for need
but for mercy. Downpour to gullywash
this rubbled knot away. May the unplanted garden
puddle and the ditch by the gravel road overrun.
Deluge. If not for mercy, to feed
the frilly azalea and the fig tree budding
and the cinnamon fern unfurling. Let me not forget
the woolly worm I saw last week in the driveway,
the dark anole sunning on the porch floor
yellowed by pollen. Whelm and sodden.
For my long-dead aunt, my namesake—or
am I hers?—years away but near. Squall. Let me
smell what's brewing. For my brother
in a hospital miles away but near. I could lose
someone. Sitting here on the steps, I watch
for hummingbirds and the first sign of a tanager.

Loosed to Canter the Wild

A wreath of bees: the hover
& hum. In long grasses, a corridor
of swishing. Something bold
has come & gone. Absence, like fire,
holds back nothing. Not loneliness.
Nor pith of withers & bones,
whatever can shoulder
what needs carriage.
Peerless, the glistening—as if wind
wrestles trees, & it does. As if, crazed,
pink petals swirl—& they do.
Let the wind shoo petals & flies.
Journey on past the farthest star,
out beyond honey & home.

Her Only

> *why then are you her only name*
> —Bruce Bond

The ghosted dorsal pen,   heronly nib. Out
the window   heronly marsh adored, much adored.

Ghosted by her only,   a marsh. The pen
her only window. A dorsal nib   adored.

~

This crested music—heronly, heronly   stream
of harmonics:

       follicles   & barbicels,
       untamed weather

Crested here   only, this stream—harmonics
her only music.

       fossil feathers,   an un-
       borrowed name

~

Barbs & barbules,   something vaned
or down. Heronly eyelashes: rictal bristles.

Her only barbs: something rictal.   Bristles
& barbules—down, down,   eyelashes down.

~

Ghosted plumage against a sky   pensive
& inked well.   So heronly, the quills.

This her only symmetry.   Quills pennaceous,
rachis unplumbed.   And what of her? Oh.

Notes

The inspiration for several poems in the book came from works of art:

"Abstractionists & Love: The Art of Forgetting": *Phenomena Prevailing Wind*, by Paul Jenkins; *Fine and Mellow*, by Michael Tyzack; *Deep Water*, by Eva Carter; *Eye of Chimu*, by Henry Botkin; *One River*, by Brian Rutenburg; *Search*, by William Halsey.

"First Sign of Bad Weather": *The Young Sailor, Icarus,* and *Sorrow of the King,* by Henri Matisse.

"Her Evening with Monet": *Port of Dieppe, Evening*, by Claude Monet.

"Dress of Flames & Upside-Down Bird": the art installation *Lesley Dill's Poetic Visions: from Shimmer to Sister Gertrude Morgan,* exhibited at the Halsey Institute, The College of Charleston, Charleston, SC, from January 25 to March 9, 2013. The poem's title is from one of the silver figures in the exhibit.

The quoted line or quoted title in each of the following poems is from *If Not, Winter: Fragments of Sappho*, translated by Anne Carson:
"*(Now Again) I Am Calling Out*"
"[on good days you would]"
"She Could Have Been a Planter Woman"
"[Let's say you forgot me]"
"Weave Such Days to a Whole"
"Her One and Only"
"You Offer Apology"
"Anytime Soon, Fall"
 "A Little Wildness"
"Anointed Yet Badly Blessed" (a quoted line & several random words)
"Late Summer"
"[Lately when sorrows come]"
"*Not one single further sorrow*"

"Hearsay" consists of letters in the author's name. "Mary Alice Alarm" consists of letters in the name *Mary Alice*.

"Spirits on the river" contains a quote by Ophelia from Shakespeare's *Hamlet*. "Virginia" in the poem refers to Virginia Woolf, who drowned herself in the Ouse River in 1941.

71

Susan Laughter (Law-ter) Meyers was the author of two collections of poems: M*y Dear, Dear Stagger Grass*, the inaugural winner of the Cider Press Review Editors' Prize, and *Keep and Give Away* (University of South Carolina Press, 2006) which received the South Carolina Poetry Book Prize, the Southern Independent Booksellers Alliance (SIBA) Book Award for Poetry, and the Brockman-Campbell Book Award. Her chapbook *Lessons in Leaving* (1998) won the Persephone Press Book Award. Her poetry has been published in numerous journals including *The Southern Review*, *Prairie Schooner*, *Beloit Poetry Journal*, *Crazyhorse*, and *jubilat*, as well as *Poetry Daily*, *Verse Daily*, and Ted Kooser's "American Life in Poetry" column. A long-time writing instructor with an MFA from Queens University of Charlotte, Meyers taught poetry workshops and classes in area community programs. She was a past president of the Poetry Societies of South Carolina and the North Carolina Poetry Society. Her awards included fellowships from the South Carolina Academy of Authors and The Virginia Center for the Creative Arts (VCCA). A North Carolina native and a resident of Summerville, South Carolina, Susan died unexpectedly on June 25, 2017. Sales from her posthumous collection, *Self-Portrait in the River of Déjà Vu*, will help support the Susan Laughter Meyers Poetry Fellowship at Weymouth from the North Carolina Poetry Society and programs with the Poetry Society of South Carolina.